NFL RECORD BREAKERS

by James Buckley, Jr.

S0-AAD-777

SCHOLASTIC INC.

New York   Toronto   London   Auckland   Sydney
Mexico City   New Delhi   Hong Kong   Buenos Aires

Visit Scholastic.com for information about our books and authors online!

ISBN 0-439-53819-X

12 11 10 9 8 7 6 5 4 3   3 4 5 6 7 8/0

Designed by Louise Bova
Printed in the U.S.A.
First Scholastic printing, August 2003

TABLE OF CONTENTS

Chapter One

PASSING INTO THE RECORD BOOKS

The National Football League (NFL) uses more numbers than a roomful of computers. There are uniform numbers, yard-line numbers, and numbers on the game clock.

Dick (Night Train) Lane

Some of the numbers are found in statistics. "Stats," as they are known, are used to show the accomplishments of the players. Comparing stats is one of every football fan's favorite hobbies. Stats are also very important to coaches and broadcasters as they prepare for games.

The players with the best stats have set all-time records, and this book is about the greatest of those records. Some all-time records have been set by superstars in today's NFL, including Jerry Rice, Emmitt Smith, and Marvin Harrison. Other records remind fans about stars of the past, such as Johnny Unitas, Jim Brown, and Dick (Night Train) Lane.

Every offensive play starts with the quarterback getting the ball, so that is where we will start. In looking over the NFL records for passing, one name stands out: Dan Marino.

Dan was a star for the Miami Dolphins from 1983 to 1999. He holds just about every career record for passing. He threw the most touchdown passes (420) and the most completions (4,967), and had the most passing yards (61,361).

Marvin Harrison

In 1984, he also set the record for most passing yards in a single season with 5,084.

Dan Marino is not the only record-setting passer, however. Along with touchdown passes and yards, the NFL ranks quarterbacks by "passer rating." This is a complicated formula that includes completion percentage and average yards per attempt.

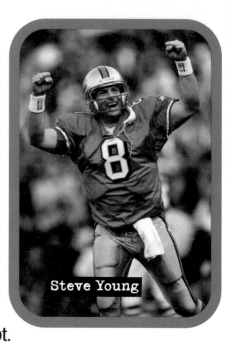

Steve Young

Dan Marino

Steve Young, who played for Tampa Bay and San Francisco, holds the career record with a 96.8 passer rating. His 112.8 rating in 1994 is also the best ever for a single season.

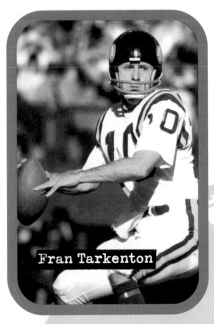

Fran Tarkenton

Steve also holds the career record for the highest pass-completion percentage, which shows how many passes he completed out of every 100 attempts. His 64.28 career percentage is the best ever. Cincinnati Bengals quarterback Ken Anderson set the single-season mark in 1982 by completing

70.55 percent of his passes. Completing passes is great, of course, but completing touchdown passes is even better. Among the players following Dan Marino on the all-time list, Fran Tarkenton, who played for the Vikings and the Giants from 1961 to 1978, is second with 342

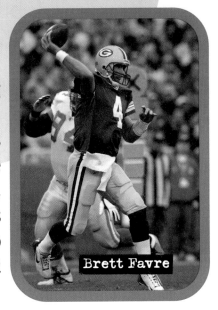

Brett Favre

touchdown passes. However, Green Bay's current passer, Brett Favre, is third with 314, and John Elway, who until 1998 was the Broncos' signal caller, is fourth with 300.

One of the greatest passing records is held by one of the

John Elway

NFL's all-time greatest players. Johnny Unitas led the Baltimore Colts for 17 seasons. From 1956 to 1960, he created perhaps the game's most unbreakable record by throwing at least one touchdown pass in 47 straight games!

Dan Marino once reached 30 straight, and no one else has even come close. "Johnny U"

Joe Montana

might not have the huge career numbers of other passers, but when the game was on the line, there was no one better.

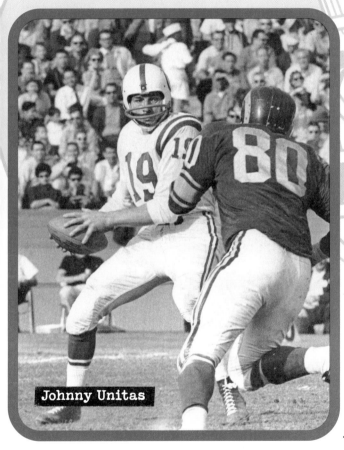

Johnny Unitas

Another great clutch passer was Joe Montana of San Francisco. Every team needs its quarterback to be at his very best during the Super Bowl, the biggest game of all, and no quarterback was more super than Joe. In four Super Bowls, he set career records for passer rating (127.8), touchdown passes (11), passing yards (1,142),

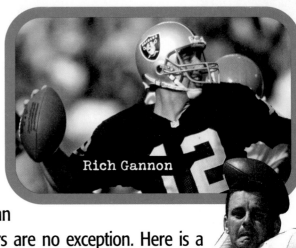

Rich Gannon

and completions (83).

It's amazing to realize what some players can do in 60 minutes (the official time of an NFL game). Passers are no exception. Here is a look at some of the best single-game passing records in NFL history.

★ In the opening game of the 1951 season, Norm Van Brocklin of the Los Angeles Rams threw for 554 yards! The second-most passing yards in one game was 527 by Warren Moon of the Houston Oilers in 1990. A good game for any NFL quarterback is 300 yards, so these were truly outstanding games.

★ In 1994, Drew Bledsoe of the Patriots completed 45 passes in an overtime game. In 2002, Rich Gannon of the Raiders set the mark for a non-overtime game with 43

Norm Van Brocklin

completions. In another 2002 game, Rich set a record by completing 21 passes in a row!

★ Five different players have thrown an astounding seven touchdown passes in one game. The first was Hall of Fame player Sid Luckman of the Chicago Bears in 1943. The New York Giants had paid tribute to Sid before the game with a special day in his honor. Sid thanked his hosts by setting the record! Joe Kapp of Minnesota was the most recent to reach the mark, in 1969.

Drew Bledsoe

★ One record that no quarterback wants to break was set by Jim Hardy of the Cardinals in a 1950 game. Poor Jim had an all-time-record eight passes intercepted! Not every record is one to write home about!

Chapter Two

RECEIVING A PLACE IN THE RECORD BOOK

This whole chapter on receiving records can be summed up in two words: Jerry Rice. With few exceptions, Jerry holds every important career and single-season receiving record. In his amazing career, which started in 1985 with San Francisco (he joined the Raiders in 2001), he has caught more passes for more yards than any player in history.

Also, if scoring touchdowns is the name of the game, you can just call this sport "JerryBall." Jerry has scored 203 touchdowns! (No other player has even reached 165.) Of those scores, 192 have come on receptions – you get one guess whether that is another all-time record!

You need a calculator just to keep up with Jerry.

Jerry Rice

Because throughout his career, he's proved that very few defenders can keep up with him any other way. Check out his distance from those in second place.

★ His total of 21,597 receiving yards is more than 5,000 yards ahead of James Lofton.

★ Jerry's 1,456 receptions put him 363 ahead of Cris Carter.

★ He has caught at least one pass in 257 games in a row — more than 60 ahead of Art Monk.

Art Monk

★ He holds the single-season records for receiving yards (1,848 in 1995) and touchdown catches (22 in 1997). Second-best on that last one? Eighteen, by Mark Clayton in 1984 and Sterling Sharpe in 1994.

Cris Carter

Oh, yes, did we mention that in four Super Bowl games, Jerry has caught more passes (33), for more yards, and more touchdowns (8) than any other player? In fact, his Super Bowl touchdown total is the most ever for any player, not just receivers!

The receiving-records section of the NFL record book should just be called the "Jerry Pages."

In 2002, Indianapolis receiver Marvin Harrison did something truly unusual: He out-Jerry-ed Jerry Rice! Until 1990, only three players in NFL history had caught 100 passes in a season. Then, in 1990, Jerry Rice caught exactly 100. In 1995, nine different players had at least 100 catches each. That season, Detroit's Herman

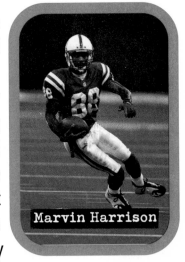

Marvin Harrison

Moore led them all with 123. Cris Carter and Jerry Rice (him again!) were second with 122. Herman's record stood until Marvin did his thing.

Herman Moore

Teaming up with quarterback Peyton Manning, Marvin shattered Moore's record (and left Rice in the dust, too) by catching an incredible 143 passes in the 2002 season! Marvin was the first draft pick of the Colts in 1996, and he has proved that they made the right choice. His 2002 total gave him 665 catches in his first seven seasons, another record. He became the first player with 100 catches in four straight seasons, breaking a record set by you-know-who and Herman Moore. It took Marvin only 102 games to reach 600 catches in his career, yet another record. It was a truly magical season.

There is another top receiver playing today who is chasing Jerry's marks. Minnesota's Randy Moss is one of the most talented athletes in the NFL. With great speed and terrific leaping ability, he has soared to the top. In 1998, he set a rookie record with 17 touchdown receptions. He is the only player with at least 1,000 receiving yards in his first four seasons. Should Jerry worry about all his records?

Time to check out the best receiving marks for a single game. Do not worry, Jerry's name comes up again here.

Terrell Owens

★ Willie (Flipper) Anderson of the Rams caught 15 passes for a record 336 yards in a 1989 game. Stephone Paige of the Chiefs is second with 309 yards in a 1985 game.

★ The most touchdown catches in one game is five. Bob Shaw of the Chicago Cardinals was the first to do it,

Kellen Winslow

in 1950. San Diego's Hall of Fame tight end Kellen Winslow matched him in 1981. And you-know-who had five in a 1990 game.

★ Terrell Owens took over for Jerry Rice as San Francisco's leading receiver. In a game in 2000, Terrell set a new record with 20 catches. He broke the record of 18 set in 1950 by Tom Fears of the Rams!

Finally, let's not leave out other players who catch passes. Shannon Sharpe, who has starred for Denver and Baltimore, is the all-time leader among tight ends with 753 catches. Among running backs, no one has caught more passes than Larry Centers, who has 808.

Shannon Sharpe

Chapter Three

RUNNING FOR RECORDS

Emmitt Smith

Emmitt Smith had to go a long way to set the all-time record for rushing yards. In 13 seasons with the Dallas Cowboys, he ran almost 10 miles! And he doesn't run in sneakers and shorts — he runs in heavy football pads and cleats, with 11 huge guys trying to stop him.

On October 27, 2002, Emmitt became the NFL's all-time leading rusher. He took over the top spot with an

Walter Payton

11-yard carry against the Seattle Seahawks. Chicago Bears great Walter Payton had been the leader with 16,726 yards, but Emmitt ran right past him. By the end of the season, Emmitt's new total was the number future backs will shoot for: 17,162 rushing yards.

Behind Emmitt and Walter is Barry Sanders of the Detroit Lions, who retired in 1998 with 15,269 yards. Barry was one of the smallest running backs in the league, but he was nearly impossible to tackle. He was as slippery as rain running down a window, and he had more moves than a stadium full of chess players.

Along with the record for most rushing yards, Emmitt must also have a very full closet. That is because he takes home every football he scores with. In 2002, he scored his 150th rushing touchdown, the most ever – that is a lot of footballs! Trailing him with 123 career rushing touch-

Terrell Davis

Eric Dickerson

downs is Marcus Allen, who starred for the Raiders and Chiefs from 1982 to 1997.

Even though Emmitt Smith has the record for most yards in a ca-

Barry Sanders

reer, the most he ever had in one season is 1,773. In 1984, Rams' running back Eric Dickerson set the mark for most yards in a season with 2,105. Only a few running backs in league history have ever topped the magic 2,000-yard mark. Among them are Barry Sanders, who had 2,053 yards in 1997, and Denver's Terrell Davis, with 2,008 in 1998.

Gaining 1,000 yards or more in a season is considered a major feat among running backs. A thousand-yard season used to be a big accomplishment. Emmitt had 11 seasons in a row with at least 1,000 yards. Barry did it 10 times, and Buffalo's Thurman Thomas racked up eight straight such seasons. (Payton had 10 thousand-yard seasons, but not in a row.)

Along with his career record, Emmitt Smith also set the mark for most rushing touchdowns in a single season. He had 25 in 1995 on his way to helping the Cowboys win another Super Bowl. John

Jim Brown

Tony Dorsett

Riggins of Washington scored 24 in 1983, and four players (including Emmitt!) have rushed for 21 scores in a season.

To figure out which running back gained the most yards per carry, you divide total yards by total carries. A good average for most running backs is about 4 yards per carry. The great Cleveland Browns running back Jim Brown holds the all-time career record with a stunning 5.22 yards per carry.

Brown is considered by some experts to be the greatest running back ever. In only nine seasons, he led the league in rushing eight times. When he retired in 1966, he was the league's all-time leading rusher with 12,312 yards. Stopping him sometimes took six or seven members of the defense.

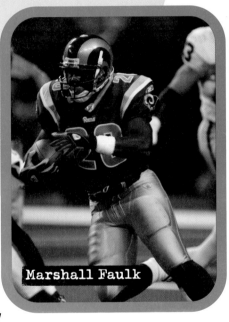

Marshall Faulk

The record for the longest run is one that can never be broken — only tied. In a 1983 *NFL Monday Night Football* game, Dallas's Tony Dorsett took off from his own one-yard line. He broke through the Vikings' line and never stopped until he had reached the end zone 99 yards away. No one can run longer be-

Corey Dillon

cause a football field is only 100 yards long!

Another way running backs earn stats is by piling up yards from scrimmage, which is figured by adding rushing yards and receiving yards. In 1999, St. Louis Rams' running back Marshall Faulk gained a record total of 2,429 yards from scrimmage.

Running backs have one of the toughest jobs in sports. Every time they touch the ball, they can plan on getting hit by at least one, but usually several, defenders. Here are some of the most successful running backs during the course of 60 hard-pounding minutes of an NFL game.

★ Cincinnati's Corey Dillon ran for 278 yards against Denver in 2000, the most ever in one game. Walter Payton's 275 yards in a 1977 game is second.

★ Ernie Nevers had a record six rushing touchdowns in one game in 1929. Jim Brown is among several others with five.

★ Gaining 200 yards in a game is pretty rare, unless you're Earl Campbell. The Houston Oilers' powerful runner had a record four 200-plus-yard games in 1980.

★ Running backs aren't the only ones who can run the ball. Atlanta's quarterback Michael Vick has the arm of John Elway and the moves of Barry Sanders. It's a dangerous combination, as the Vikings found out in 2002. Vick set a new single-game record for rushing yards by a quarterback with 173. His per-carry average of 17.3 yards broke a 52-year-old record held by Hall of Fame running back Marion Motley.

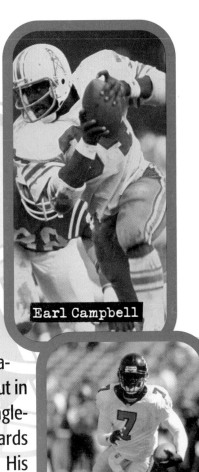

Earl Campbell

Michael Vick

Chapter Four

DEFENDING THEIR RECORDS

Defensive players rack up stats, too. The best known defensive stat is the interception. This happens when a defender catches a pass meant for an offensive player. A defender then returns the interception for as many yards as he can, sometimes even scoring. Players and coaches know that creating turnovers (interceptions and fumbles) is often one of the keys to victory.

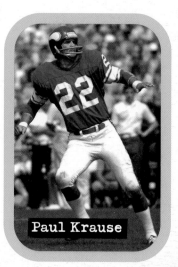

Paul Krause

The all-time interceptions leader is Paul Krause, who snagged 81 from 1964 to 1979 for Washington and Minnesota. New York Giants' great Emlen Tunnell is next with 79. In third place is a fa-

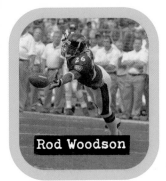

Rod Woodson

miliar face to today's NFL fans. Rod Woodson has played for Pittsburgh, Baltimore, and Oakland in a career that is sure to land him in the Hall of Fame. Woodson reached a career total of 69 interceptions with an AFC-leading 8 in 2002. His 2 touchdowns on interception returns extended his all-time record to 12 touchdowns. He also jumped over Tunnell to finish the season with a career-record 1,465 interception return yards.

Dick (Night Train) Lane's 14 interceptions in 1952 is not only still the single-season record, it is also the record for rookies. Night Train was a Hall of Fame player for three teams from 1952 to 1965. The record for interceptions in one game is 4, held by many players. Denver's Deltha O'Neal did it most recently in 2001.

Another way defenses can turn around a game – and make

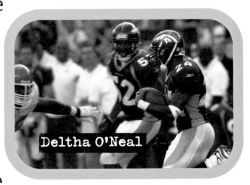

Deltha O'Neal

their mark in the record book – is with the sack. A sack happens when the quarterback is tackled behind the line of scrimmage (the place where each play starts). Defenders – usually linemen and linebackers – use moves, speed, and strength to get around blockers and tackle the passer.

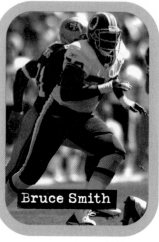

Bruce Smith

Sacks have been an official stat since 1982. Since then, the all-time leader is Reggie White, who played for

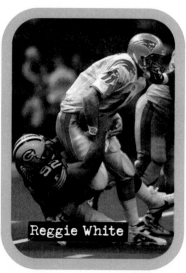

Reggie White

the Eagles, Packers, and Panthers from 1985 to 2000. Reggie's total of 198 is just three more than Bruce Smith, who first played for the Bills and now lines up for the Redskins. Both players are defensive ends.

The single-season record was set in 2001 by the Giants' Michael Strahan. He had 22.5 sacks. How do you get 0.5 (one-half) of a sack? Good

Michael Strahan

question. When two players tackle the quarterback behind the line, they each get 0.5 of a sack.

Only one player has notched seven sacks in one game: Kansas City's great linebacker Derrick Thomas. He sacked Seattle's quarterback that many times in a 1990 game.

One other defensive stat is worth mentioning. If a defense's job is to stop the other team from scoring, no one did that better than the 1932 Chicago Bears. They allowed only 44 points in 14 games, the lowest single-season total ever. It would be fun to see how Chicago's "Monsters of the Midway" of the old days would do against today's high-flying, record-setting offenses.

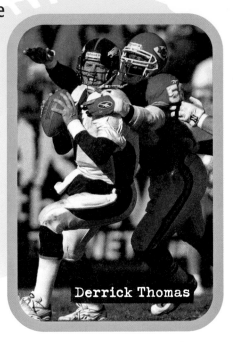

Derrick Thomas

Chapter Five

KICKING UP THE RECORDS

Kickers do not get much glory, but everyone re-members them when they miss an important kick! Because they get credit for field goals and point-after-touchdown kicks, kickers hold most of the scoring records. In 21 seasons, Gary Anderson, with Min-nesota in 2002, scored a record 2,223 points. He also holds the all-time record with 494 field goals. Trailing him slightly at 2,153 points is Morten Andersen, most recently with the Chiefs. Morten's 486 field goals are also the second-most ever.

Gary Anderson

Olindo Mare of Miami banged through a single-season record 39 field goals in 1999.

Olindo Mare

John Kasay's 37 for Carolina in 1996 is second-best. Three players hold the record for most field goals in a game with seven. Dallas kicker Chris Boniol went seven-for-seven in a 1996 game.

What about longest? Only a handful of today's kickers are very successful at more than 50 yards. Morten Andersen holds the all-time record for such kicks with 39. However, two players have booted field goals that flew a record 63 yards. The first was Tom Dempsey of the

Tom Dempsey

Saints, who kicked his in 1970. (He was born with only half of a right foot and used a special flat-front shoe to make his kicks.) In 1998, Jason Elam of Denver matched Dempsey's mark.

A player who combined kicking and running skills holds the all-time single-season record for points

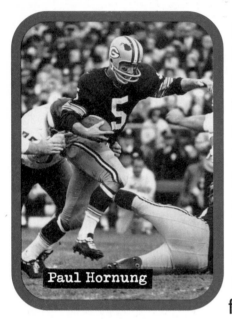

Paul Hornung

scored. Green Bay's Paul Hornung was not only a talented runner, he was also the team's kicker! In 1960, he scored 176 points by scoring 15 touchdowns, kicking 15 field goals, and converting 41 point-after-touchdown kicks.

Finally, the greatest one-man gang in football history was Ernie Nevers. In a game for the Chicago Cardinals in 1929, he scored an amazing 40 points! The Hall of Fame running back ran for six touchdowns and added four extra-point kicks. (Two other players have scored six touchdowns in a game.)

It is great to read about the amazing records set by decades of NFL stars. But what is also great about the NFL is watching this season's games to see when the next records will be set. Who knows . . . it could happen this Sunday!